Number Fun

Written by Charlotte Raby
and Emily Guille-Marrett
Illustrated by Laura González

Collins

1

2

3

2

1–5

1–10

8

9

1–10

12

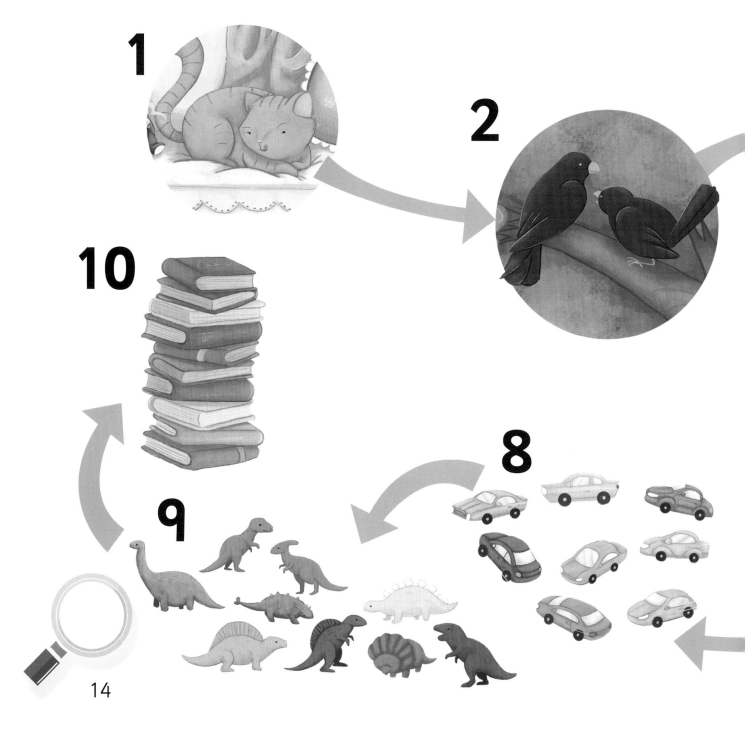

3

4

5

7

6

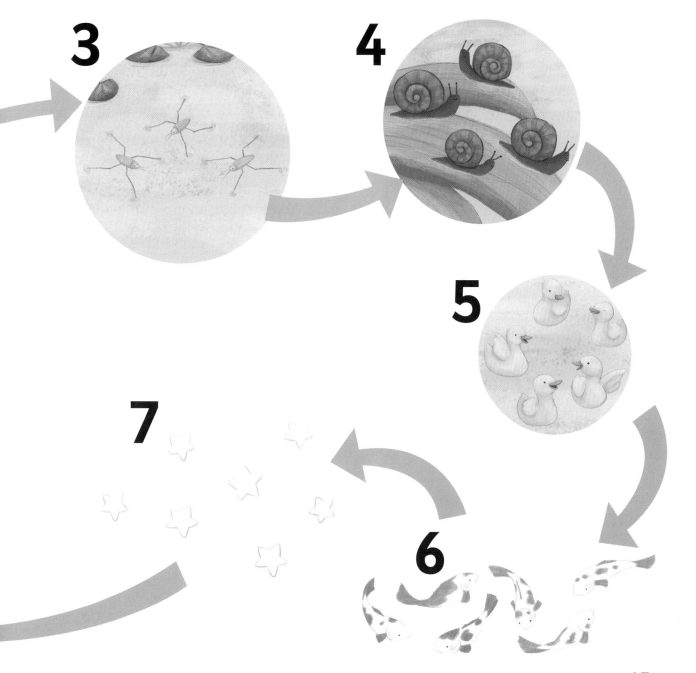

 After reading

Letters and Sounds: Phase 1
Word count: 0
Curriculum links: Understanding the World: The World
Early learning goals: Listening and attention: Listen to stories, accurately anticipating key events and respond to what is heard with relevant comments, questions or actions; Understanding: answer 'how' and 'why' questions about experiences and in response to stories or events

Developing fluency

- Encourage your child to hold the book the right way up and turn the pages.
- Let them explore the pages and tell you their version of the 'story', using the pictures for support.

Phonic practice

- Say the sounds in the words below. Ask your child to repeat the sounds and then say the word.

  b/e/d   bed   c/a/t   cat   c/u/p   cup

  t/e/d   ted   d/u/ck   duck

- If your child cannot work out what the word is, say the sounds, and then say the word. Ask your child to repeat after you.
- Challenge your child to find amounts of each object in the story, e.g. two teds.

Extending vocabulary

- Look at the pages showing the pond on pages 6–9. Ask your child to point to the animals and insects in the pictures. Can your child name any of the animals? (e.g. *duck, snail, frog*)
- Look at the animals and discuss which animals/insects can live in the water and which live on land.
- Talk about the relative size of the animals/insects. Use the words: 'bigger', 'smaller', 'biggest', 'smallest', 'largest' etc. to help your child describe their relative sizes.
- Talk about the unusual language in the different nursery rhymes. Some nursery rhymes have made up words like 'Hickory, dickory, dock'. What other words can your child make up?